Contents

Acknowledgements 4
Section 1: Selling is an Awful Lot Like Fishing 7
    What kind of fish do you want? 7
    Where are these fish? 7
    How to catch these fish? 8
Section 2: Buying is a Lot Like Being a Fish in Water 10
    Are the fish looking for your bait? 10
    Do you have what it takes to reel the fish in? 10
    You caught the fish. Now what? 11
Section 3: The Basics 12
    Compensation Plan 12
    Sales Quota 12
    Sales Territory 12
    Commission 13
    Accelerators 13
Section 4: The Buying and Selling Processes in Detail 14
    The Buying Process 14
        Need Awareness 14
        Need Definition 15
        Solution Research 15
        Evaluation of Alternatives 15
        Need Alignment 16
        Negotiation 16
        Purchase Decision / Close 17
        Implementation 17
        Post-Purchase Evaluation 17

- The Selling Process 18
    - Profile 18
    - Prospect 18
    - Gain Access 19
    - Intake and Identify Opportunity 19
    - Align the Value 19
    - Paint the Picture 20
    - Propose 20
    - Re-Align 20
    - Decide / Close 20
    - Support 21
- Sales Qualification 21
    - Budget 23
    - Method 23
    - Authority 24
    - Need 25
    - Timing 25
    - Risk 26
- Section 5: Do Not Be Your Own Worst Enemy 26
    - They like you 27
    - They believe in the value that will come from your product or service 27
    - How to leverage the value wedge 30
    - They trust you 30
- Section 6: Asking Questions 31
    - Share with me 31
    - Tell me about 31
    - Explain to me 31

2

- Walk me through 31
- Describe for me 32

Section 6: The Best Leads 33
- Marketing Support 34
- Decision Makers and Influencers 35
  - Decision informants 35
  - Decision influencers 35
  - Decision makers 35
- Bottom up versus top down 35
- Bottom up 36
- Top down 36

Section 7: Now Go Win 37
- Do not whine 37
- Do not put yourself in a position to blame others 38
- Find a mentor and a mentee 38
- Avoid negative people 38
- Choose a personal goal and justify your career towards that goal 39
- Outwork your competition 39
- Put yourself in the shoes of your buyer 40

Acknowledgements

I must begin by thanking my father, Richard for taking a leap of faith and coming to America at just 16 years old. Thank you for teaching me how to sell with a smile and to put your customers first.

Thanks to my mother, Norma for helping him run the company for the last 20+ years.

Thank you to my wife, Analisa for your patience and for taking such good care of our children.

Thank you to Jennifer Atiyeh for editing this book.

The Last Sales Book

In the sea of books about sales, it is challenging to find one that cuts through the noise and speaks to the foundation of what selling is all about. I have decided to write this book for a few reasons. The primary of which is for use in a sales course I teach at The University of Portland. Beginning in 2013, I have used myriad sales books and have found myself frequently correcting the author and interpreting various passages on behalf of my students. Additionally, as a ten-year sales professional whose worked for companies large and small, I've been asked or required to read some of these books. From a go-to-market perspective, the various messages these books communicate become the flavor of the month and quickly fizzle away as individual sellers revert to their own sales methodology. I have two core observations: first, if your pipeline was full and you were at or above your sales quota, you were free to ignore these books. Lastly, those who embraced these books and practiced what was preached do not become better sellers overnight. It takes a commitment to the principals espoused by the author. The overwhelming output became simply one thing: a sales process.

Organizations are spending several weeks and thousands of dollars training salespeople on selling their product using their methodology and tools. My class produces sales-oriented young professionals who can help reduce these expenses. I have realized without a book that purports a clean selling methodology, I am unable to fully realize this goal.

One reason many books about sales exist is there simply is no silver bullet to sales success. No single book can communicate the *right* way to sell. There are too many variables for any one sales process to take into consideration. Some of those variables are less complex than the biggest variable, which is *people*. Yes, when we sell, we sell to people. Human beings are complicated and cannot be predicted. As sellers develop and leverage a sales process with consistency, the complexity and variability of human buyers does not follow suit. This book attempts to reduce the noise and communicate the basic elements of the selling and buying processes to build your own individual style upon a solid and proven foundation.

Section 1: Selling is an Awful Lot Like Fishing

If you wake up one day and feel like going fishing, but you have never fished before, you will be in for quite a shock when you arrive at the river. You may catch one fish or several, or you may not catch anything at all. If you do not catch a fish you may ask, "why am I so bad at this?". If you do catch a fish you may say "this is easy!", and in either case a highly successful fisherperson would question your approach. Did you have the right rod or bait? Did you go at the right time? Did you know the kind of fish you wanted to catch? To understand this better, let us unpack this further.

What kind of fish do you want?

Fishing: The very first thing a fisherperson does is decide what kind of fish they want to catch. Perhaps they require large fish that have a lot of meat. They would need to catch one of these fish to feed them and their family for a month. It may be the case the fisherperson does not have access to these large fish. So, they choose to fish in small lakes with small fish. In that case they need to catch a dozen small fish as they have less meat on them. Large fish do not belong in small ponds and small trout fish do not belong in the ocean. The fisherperson may decide upon their ideal fish based on their geography and access to particular waters.

Selling: A salesperson must know their ideal customer. This can be obtained by looking at existing customers with tenure and high satisfaction surveys. If the salesperson is an entrepreneur starting a new business, it is important to build a buyer profile or persona that has all the demographics of an ideal customer: revenue, employee size, city/state/country, etc. Knowing what kind of companies you want to sell to will help orient your approach to how those companies buy. More on this later.

Where are these fish?

Fishing: If the fisherperson has access to small lakes and ponds they will spend their time fishing there. If they have a large family to feed they will need a lot of fish. Regardless, if their family can survive on these fish at that volume and the local lakes and ponds support that, there is no reason to leave the area in search of new fish or larger bodies of water. The fisherperson will document the waters around them by size and distance from home. The same is true of the fisherperson seeking the large fish. They will identify the large waters and oceans nearest to them.

Selling: The salesperson, knowing the demographics of their ideal buyers, will go where those buyers are located. Unlike fish, buyers have addresses. But, like fish, they may be in clusters (city centers and business parks). If the salesperson understands the market(s) where his buyers are located there is no reason to call on buyers who do not meet the defined profile.

How to catch these fish?

Fishing: The fisherperson will now try to catch the fish. First, they must consider several things:

- Where exactly are these fish, relative to the body of water they are swimming in? Are they swimming shallow or deep?
- When do these fish rise from the bottom of the water to eat? Do they like to swim when the sun is low, medium or high? Do they prefer nighttime?
- What kind of bait do the fish like?
- Do you have the right rod that can cast far enough and strong enough to reel in the fish?

Let's assume the fisherperson does not have access to other successful fisherpersons who can answer these questions. The fisherperson must then assume and subsequently attempt to catch fish. It may take some experimentation, but the fish will bite on a limited set of bait. The bait used on large fish would not work on small fish. It may take several days to experiment with the assumptions the fisherperson has made. Another layer of complexity: the results of these experiments may vary by the seasons of the year due to externalities that affect the bodies of water the fisherperson is hunting in.

Selling: The salesperson must also choose an approach and is facing questions of their own:

- What are the exact locations of my buyers? Where do they conduct their research?
- When do your buyers conduct research online versus reading whitepapers or attending seminars?
- What kind of benefits your product or service offers will trigger your buyer?
- Is the buyer going to be compelled by your messaging (emails, LinkedIn messages, cold calls)?

Section 2: Buying is a Lot Like Being a Fish in Water

Have you ever experienced a sudden realization that you have a problem? I certainly have. I recall watching NBA commentary on YouTube when between videos a commercial for a gaming mouse piqued my interest. I found myself questioning if I had been depriving myself of a more comfortable experience on my home PC setup. From this example we can extend our metaphor of the fisherperson and the salesperson.

Are the fish looking for your bait?

Fishing: Now that the fisherperson has determined a plan to approach the fish and the body of water with all their gear and bait in tow, it is time to put it to the test. He strolls up to the water in the morning and casts a line deep with insects as his bait. And now he waits for the first bite of the day.

Selling: The salesperson has a similar arsenal. When they put themselves in the intersection of their sales collateral and the buyer, they are testing this approach. They are looking for a buyer to "bite". The engagement that results from that bite can be a verbal conversation, email or direct message exchange. In either case, it is a bite, not a sale.

If a large portion of your buyers do not express interest in your messaging, it would make sense trying something new. Caution: do not change more than one thing at a time. You do not know what you have wrong here. It may not be your messaging. It could be your buyer profile is inaccurate. For example, you may be targeting the office of finance when you should be targeting information technology (IT). Or, perhaps, you should be targeting director level instead of executive level. Make one change and try again.

Do you have what it takes to reel the fish in?

Fishing: Fish on! The fisherperson has fish on the line and now it is time to reel it in. This is a combination of patience and strength. Moreover, it is about knowing when to reel and how hard to tug at the line. Smaller fish are easy to win over. They do not have the strength to put up much of a fight so the process of reeling them in is shorter than with a large fish.

Selling: The salesperson is engaged with the buyer and now must read the buyer's signals to understand how to qualify whether they are the right kind of buyer. If they are a qualified buyer, meaning they have budget, understand their needs and have a sense of timing, the seller has a chance to progress the engagement to closure.

Knowing how to react here is a very human experience. People reveal signs of buying both verbally and non-verbally. They will also show you if they like you or not – and this is a critical requirement of buyers.

You caught the fish. Now what?

Fishing: It is time to eat that fish. The fisherperson now has the fish in hand and must skin it, cook it, distribute it and eat it until it is gone. It may be too difficult to skin or transport. Or it could be unhealthy or even poisonous!

Selling: The salesperson has closed the deal and now it is time to deliver on the commitments that were made during the sales process. Ultimately the scope outlined in the contract will reign, but buyers remember what the salesperson committed verbally.

Precisely how you deliver and manage your customer will effect your reputation.

Section 3: The Basics

Salespeople are contractually motivated to sell. They are provided a compensation plan, quota target and territory. Some sales positions also offer a base salary. An entry level sales role may offer a total 12-month compensation for reaching quota at around $50,000. For seasoned sales professionals, they are more likely to earn upwards of $200,000 as a field representative. The elite sales professionals are, of course, making much more. Learning how to maximize your compensation plan will help you understand which products or services are most lucrative. You may learn how to stack products together to further amplify your earnings. It all starts with learning the basics.

Compensation Plan

The compensation plan (sometimes referred to as an "incentive plan") is the underlying logic for sales commission payouts. Ultimately these plans dictate the behavior of the sales representative. They address base salary, sales goals, commission percentages, incentives and any non-cash rewards related to sales performance. Examples of non-cash rewards include company stock or eligibility for company funded trips. The latter is often referred to as "President's Club."

Sales Quota

A sales quota is the numeric target the sales representative must hit to be considered satisfactory in their work function. A sales quota can be measured in dollar booking targets or a unit measurement. The time periods include monthly, quarterly or annually.

Sales Territory

A sales territory is the boundary in which the sales representative can offer their product or service. This is outlined often as a geographical region but can also be addressed by the demographics of the target customers. Some territories are strictly a list of companies the seller may work with. And they can be in the same market or geographical region as other sellers on their team. For example, a territory may be all for-profit companies with annual revenue greater than $10 million in the state of Oregon.

Commission

Commission is the actual payout received by the sales representative for their performance. Commission will have a payout schedule attached to it. Commission can be complicated. For example, if the average deal size is $100,000 with a 10% commission, the employer is accustomed to this. But when the seller closes a deal that is well above the norm, such as $1,000,000, it may yield a commission that is too large for the employer. In which case the commission may have a cap or a special payout schedule. Instead of a single payment it may be several payments over time. Note: often the sales representative needs to be employed during the payout period in order to receive their commission.

Commission plans are rarely negotiable and are not always achievable. An experienced salesperson will closely review a commission plan before accepting it or seek new employment if an existing plan is replaced by a plan he finds unacceptable.

Accelerators

Accelerators are additional motivators that provide a multiplicative effect on the standard commission plan. For example, an employer may choose to motivate sellers to promote the sale of a particular product, so they add an accelerator to it that pays double after a certain unit or dollar booking target is reached.

Section 4: The Buying and Selling Processes in Detail

To understand how to best position your content, it is critical to understand the steps a buyer makes as they enter and exit the buying process. Furthermore, in understanding buying behavior, marketers can better interpret the various mouse clicks, form submissions and downloads that buyers go through. This allows for buyer personas to be created and behavior scoring algorithms and rules to have meaning and purpose in the overall marketing strategy. Consequently, it gives marketers the ability to measure the value of actions as they relate to a particular product or service, as well as represent the value of marketing during the general marketing and demand generation cycles.

The Buying Process

Consumers undergo a buying process before they walk out of the store with their new vacuum or drive off the dealership with their new car. This is the buying process. Returning to the fishing metaphor, the fish may observe the bait laid by the fisherperson but they may not like that type of bait or are not hungry at the time.

Need Awareness

Typically, there is a trigger for the buyer when they become aware of a need. Trigger sources include the economy, leadership changes and outside perspectives, competition and sometimes things just break. The buyer may not immediately move on to the next step. It is not always the decision maker that becomes aware of the need. A standard sales qualification procedure is to ask the necessary questions to learn if there is support for a buying process by the decision maker(s).

Example) The instrument cluster in your car fails.

Need Definition

It is common for a buyer to quantify the gap they need to fill or the issues they are experiencing. A business need may be anything from replacing an employee (hiring is a lot like buying) to acquiring a business.

Example continued) You have defined your need as needing to read your odometer. Noting your speedometer and fuel gadget are fully functional.

Solution Research

This step refers to the actions taken to find a solution to the need. Typical activities include meeting with salespeople, product demonstrations, trials and proofs of concept.

Example continued) You take your car to a shop and discover the cost of repair is $2,000. The overall value of your car is $9,000.

Evaluation of Alternatives

Buyers will compare their options before choosing a leading option. An alternative to buying is to not buy anything at all. But acting is just as common.

Example continued) You determine you have three options:

1. Repair the odometer ($2,000) – effectively devaluing your car 22%.
2. Sell your car and buy something new, as the repair costs are too high relative to the value of your car. A more expensive proposition.
3. Choose not to repair your car (not acting).

Need Alignment

It is not uncommon for a buyer to make concessions to find the best solution to their need. This alignment period may include weeks of internal meetings where the pros and cons are discussed, quantified and prioritized.

Example continued) To finalize your decision you consult friends and family (trusted advisors) and ask what they would do. You want to know if their opinion comes from a place of experience and is something you can trust. You are given some additional information to help reach a decision: before the odometer went out, your car was at 70,000 miles. Your car's manufacturer recommends a significant service at 75,000 miles and you learn it will cost $1,100. Furthering the devaluation of your vehicle.

Negotiation

This occurs immediately upon viewing the seller's proposal. Commonly negotiated terms include price/rate, scope of work, duration of service and start dates. These are later referred to as *levers of complexity*.

Example continued) You decide to drive the car for another 6-8 months before selling it. If a good deal comes your way (price) you may bite earlier (start date). You begin the negotiation process by informing a few key dealers that you are in the market. You have defined your need, which is now more than a functioning odometer. You describe the vehicle you want and your timeline (6-8 months). As time passes, a vehicle you would like to buy comes your way. You begin formal negotiation about the purchase price, loan amount, loan rate, loan duration and trade in value of your vehicle. The dealer presumes the repair cost of your trade in vehicle to be exactly $2,000 less than street value because of the needed repair. You negotiate based on your repair being a cost basis for the dealership rather than a bill basis. Also, there would not be a markup on the procured replacement parts.

Purchase Decision / Close

A purchase decision is the formalization of the purchase by signing contracts. Documents may include non-disclosure agreements, services agreements and statements of work.

Example continued) With the dealer having met most of your terms, you make the decision to purchase the new vehicle. They provide you with the need to execute, as well as the loan and title information.

Implementation

This represents the period after all contracts have been signed and filed. At this point, the buyer may need to configure software or become oriented with a service. Perhaps even both. This stage may last anywhere from hours to months to years. It may be a rollout over time with multiple phases. It is possible a future phase may be at risk, from a sales perspective, if the previous phase(s) are not delivered successfully.

Example continued) You have been handed the keys and drive the car off the lot. You orient yourself to the vehicle.

Post-Purchase Evaluation

This is a challenging period for the buyer as remorse can set in if they do not experience value from their decision. As a seller, you can limit this risk by asking the right questions about the buyer's needs and tuning your product or service to align best with those needs.

Example continued) You find the vehicle to have more enjoyable features and more comfort, but the feel of the road has changed. The technology in this vehicle takes getting used to. It is not as fun as your previous car.

The Selling Process

As stated in the Buying Cycle, there is a methodology a buyer implements before ultimately transacting. The Selling Process is another methodology for salespeople to follow. In business to business sales, the cycle lasts weeks, months or years long. It is easier to identify each part of the process. In business to customer sales, the cycle is often much shorter, making the process more difficult to identify. Regardless, it does exist. A knowledge of the selling process helps marketers understand how their counterparts in sales observe their opportunity cycles and how potential customers can be courted.

Profile

To help ensure success in later steps, one should pursue only the prospective customers who would be a good fit for their product or service. For example, software that only supports English may not be a good fit for companies that have 90% Spanish-speaking employees. Another more simplistic example is one should not try to sell an Alfa Romero sportscar to a teenager without a job.

Example continued) You work for a financial advisor and are incentivized to acquire new customers. They are profiled as middle-aged with at least $500,000 in assets and little debt. They are beginning to think more strategically about their retirement strategy.

Prospect

Gaining the attention of prospective customers is a difficult activity. This is a great step for a Marketing department that specializes in getting the attention of prospects. Activities include an informative whitepaper and case study distribution, as well as hosting webinars and educational events. An individual sales professional can leverage local groups for professionals or social media to specifically target a prospect.

Example continued) You spend the majority of your day calling prospects that received a mailer from your company. You make 30-50 calls each.

Gain Access

This represents the first business meeting with the seller and buyer. The seller should aim to build rapport with the buyer, understand the buying criteria and steps, as well as secure a next step.

Example continued) During a call, the prospect answers, acknowledges receiving the mailer and agrees to a follow up meeting with one of your advisors.

Intake and Identify Opportunity

Before a sale can take place, the seller needs to capture the buying requirements. This can be a significant investment for both parties. And a major contributor to deal qualification. If a customer is willing to invest the time necessary to fully convey their requirements and the seller or sales team perform well, the likelihood of a transaction increases. Furthermore, the customer is more likely to be satisfied after the implementation.

Example continued) During the meeting, the advisor walks the prospect through a questionnaire that help identify what the prospect's needs are.

Align the Value

Following an intake, the sales professional can build the value statement and win theme. A value statement is the foundation of the buyer's decision to partner with the seller. A win theme is a layer of detail beyond the value statement that captures, at a high level, the justification the buyer would need to approve partnering with the seller.

Example continued) The win themes are articulated to be "a strong customer service team" and "the speed of implementation".

Paint the Picture

Prior to formalizing the levers of complexity behind the sales transaction the seller must help the buyer visualize what business would look like with the seller's product or service in place. This can be a proof of concept, demonstration or complex workflow.

Example continued) Before a contract is presented, a proposal is given to the customer that is light on legal terms and heavy on details regarding the product or service solves the customer's problem.

Propose

The proposal step is the formal expression of a sales offering for the buyer. This is typically delivered in written form.

Example continued) The sales professional meets with the prospect to walk through the contract.

Re-Align

After your initial proposal the negotiation begins. As the customer negotiates on terms the salesperson or team will conform their offering to meet the prospect's requirements.

Example continued) The sales professional meets again with the customer after making changes to the contract per the prospect's request.

Decide / Close

When a buyer makes a decision, it is accounted for in this step as the formalization of the purchase decision by executing contracts. Salespeople refer to this decision as a "close". Supporting documents may include non-disclosure agreements, services agreements and statements of work. This step maps to buying cycle step named *Purchase Decision*.

Example continued) Signatures are captured and filed internally. In turn, the client support or service team come together with the Sales team to plan how to get the customer serviced.

Support

Customer support is an ongoing stage, differing between a paid engagement or volunteer based. A software sales representative, for example, can further the likelihood of an upsell by checking in with the customer every several weeks and helping escalate issues the customer may have. Purchase decisions are influenced by the relationship between buyers and sellers. Strong sellers maintain this relationship. There is always the possibility the customer's expectations are not being met. It is the responsibility of the sales professional to ensure they are. In many organizations, the onus shifts from Sales to another team, such as Customer Service. I contend, the reputation of the sales professional is his or her most important asset and they should strive to protect this by working with the customer and the service and support teams to ensure the customer is happy.

Example continued) The prospect, now a customer, is struggling to understand how her money is being managed. She calls support weekly to get assistance, which is beyond expectation. Client Support contacts the sales professional who steps in to speak with the customer about their service.

Sales Qualification

As the sales cycle progresses, the seller is putting more time into the opportunity. To justify this time and to validate progress, the practice of sales qualification is used. The methodology behind determining if an opportunity is qualified is called BMANTR, which is an acronym that stands for the six most important attributes of an opportunity: Budget, Method, Authority, Need, Timing and Risk. As an opportunity progresses from Stage 1 (Identify Need) all the way to Stage 7 (Close), more information is learned about the opportunity. BMANTR does not supersede or circumvent a sales methodology. It is a compliment to a sales process. BMANTR is meant to augment the qualification process and help guide the salesperson and marketing team to ask better and more insightful questions. It should be implemented throughout the sales cycle, following primary or secondary customer education and can serve as a necessary progress check throughout the sales cycle. A good sales manager wants to know the customer's budget and timing. Within marketing campaigns, it is possible to learn some of this information as well.

Benefits of BMANTR include some of the following:

- Provides a qualification method to address the six key deal criteria that are necessary in any qualified deal that can be leveraged by salespeople, presales, consulting, sales management, et al.
- Provides criteria to measure and manage investment based on how many or how completely questions are answered.
- Provides criteria to judge level of detail, quality and consistency of information received throughout the sales cycle.
- Provides a baseline for give-gets when we negotiate with information prior to spending resources and discussing price.
- Provides a "vernacular" that can regulate conversations between salespeople and sales management to drive fact-based conversation, reduce emotion, eliminate filibustering and increase efficiency that can leveraged day to day or in any exercises that tie to operational discipline (e.g. Weekly One on One Meetings, Territory Reviews, etc.).

- It can help win deals, forecast more effectively, manage investments; abandon sales opportunities that appear to be an upcoming loss.
- Value is predicated on the quality of executing the BMANTR questioning, not just going through the motions. Garbage information in = garbage out.

Below are some examples of how to use BMANTR:

Budget

What is the budget allocated to fill the stated need? This may change during the cycle if the need expands or contracts.

- Has budget been identified and expressly earmarked for this purchase, or is this a part of a broader category buy (e.g. Quote to Cash Initiative)? What are the dependencies?
- Who owns this budget? Is this different than the individual that is being given permission to exercise this budget?
- What is the customers budgeting cycle?
- Are there any other special requirements around the money, aka, is there a trigger to approve and release funds?
- Are there any international currency implications that need to be addressed?

Method

How will the customer evaluate a solution to their need? Who are the people involved and where are they located?

- What are the evaluation criteria for determining if these capabilities are required?
- What are the evaluation criteria for technology selection?
- How do we measure success? Who determines success? Do we need to have this documented and agreed to with the customer?
- Who determines that the completed work needs on the program and deems it meritorious for funding?
- How are you going to configure, deploy, evaluate and decide on this?
- What are the needed roles in this process? How do they work together to assist the lead sales representative? How can sales leadership support the sale? What are the resource requirements? Are there other investments?
- What is the decision method? Email, meeting, with whom? When is this scheduled for? Has this expectation been set?
- Is a business case required to get the deal fully executed? What constitutes this? Are there other examples?

Authority

Ultimately, who will sign the contract?[3]

- Who at the end of the day needs to say yes to this (not just IT, the Sponsor)?
- Who can say no?
- Have we met these people and confirmed that it is their intent to procure these capabilities?
- Who are the technical decision makers, and the business decision makers?

- Is the decision maker the same person that owns the budget with profit and loss?
- How is approval granted, are there multiple approvers?
- If this is a departmental decision, does someone from the larger business have to be briefed and sign off?

Need

What is the defined need and business value?

- Why do they need this solution? What is the business or operational value? What is the gap this addresses?
- Can the need be quantified into a Total Cost of Ownership (TCO) or Return on Investment (ROI)? Do we know the business case? Have we participated in its development?
- Is this an expressed explicit need (part of a requirements document for the program that customer needs to meet), or an implicit need?
- How does this need map to the success of the company?
- Is the decision maker tied into this need?
- What is the cost of doing nothing? What are the risks?

Timing

When does the customer expect to start a solution and realize value?

- If we understand why, and why us, then why now?
- What is the timeframe communicated for selection, decision and procurement? Has this expectation been set? How are we managing to this date? Do we have an agreed upon plan for

evaluating the product or service being sold? Has that plan been confirmed with the opportunity sponsor?
- If this slips by the XXX timeframe, what other than our communicated terms effected? What is driving this timeframe for this to get procured, deployed? Funding availability, program schedule, need?
- Have we driven a compelling event to reinforce the customers? Have we implemented a before/after proposal in place that we have discussed and confirmed with the customer?

Risk

What are the risks associated with not closing the deal?

- Direct and indirect (variable) risk? What is the risk if this is not getting done?
- What could make or prevent your deal from closing?
- Competitive? Competing initiatives? Political? Timing?

Section 5: Do Not Be Your Own Worst Enemy

One theme of this book is putting effort into what is within your control while understanding outside influences or externalities that impact your likelihood to win. You can follow the sales process perfectly but if the buyer does not like you – something you control – you reduce your likelihood of closing the deal. There are three reasons people buy:

1. They like you
2. They believe in the value that will come from your product or service

3. They trust you

They like you

In my time selling I never had an issue with #1. My buyers always liked me because I am respectful, caring and I listen to them. It was not a challenge for me to engage with someone I did not know and over time establish a great rapport. Here are a few tips to help you be likable:

- Smile often
- Always be polite and courteous
- Let the buyer talk
- Give value before you ask for their business
- Do not talk about religion or politics with your buyer

My parents ingrained these principals in me without beating me over the head with them. My dad, an entrepreneur since age sixteen ran his business for fifty years before retiring in early 2019. He did not use analytics or track any key performance indicators. He did not have sales goals or even employees. He and my mother ran their business for the final twenty years and their business was mostly repeat customers who wanted to engage with them while shopping for plants and shrubs. In other words, the buyers *liked* my parents. Being likable affords sellers some amount of grace. As you enter a sales cycle with a business that is new to you, you are interacting with people who often are quite familiar with that business. There is no way you can walk in and know more than they do; yet sellers are often the experts in their own products and services, causing them to display over-confidence. I have seen this move more times than I can count: the seller says "yes" to everything the buyer says. The seller does not just say it in response to "can your software do this?" but also for trivial, getting-to-know-you questions such as "did you see the game last night?". The risk here is not being liked when eventually your white lie becomes exposed. Be smart and be honest; this will make you more likable.

They believe in the value that will come from your product or service

Communicating value to a buyer is one of the simpler tasks that most sales professionals mess up. One of the best managers I ever had told me: make it easy for people to say, "yes". What he meant is to keep it simple. It is easy to overcomplicate a sales cycle. Again, this comes back to variables and what is and what is not within your control as a seller. What is within your control is asking your customer to explain their perception of their need. What is also within your control is explaining to your customer what your product or service offers. There are features of your product or service that when matched your customer's needs creates value. This is why it is critical to maintain your reputation as a likable person who brings value to his or her customers: your customers will be your best lead generators. More on this in Section 6.

Many sales managers and trainers I have had over the years have repeated the same misperception of our competitors: never mention them. This is a bad rule. Think about it and keep it simple: your competitors exist because there are buyers out there with the same needs you are trying to address. If that is not an excellent endorsement of your product or service then I do not know what is. I am not advocating you wear your competitor's hats or use pens with their logo on it, rather, I am advocating you do not shy away from understanding them so well that you cannot have a real conversation with your buyers about why your offering is going to provide more value, I if you do not feel confident that your offering is the best for the buyers you have identified then you need to either revisit the buyer profiles or you need to get a job with the competition.

Once you are engaged with your buyer regarding the validity of your competition, I recommend you run them through this exercise. The exercise, called *The Value Wedge* developed by [Corporate Visions](), has been modified for use as a selling exercise. Before I explain how to use it, observe what it is:

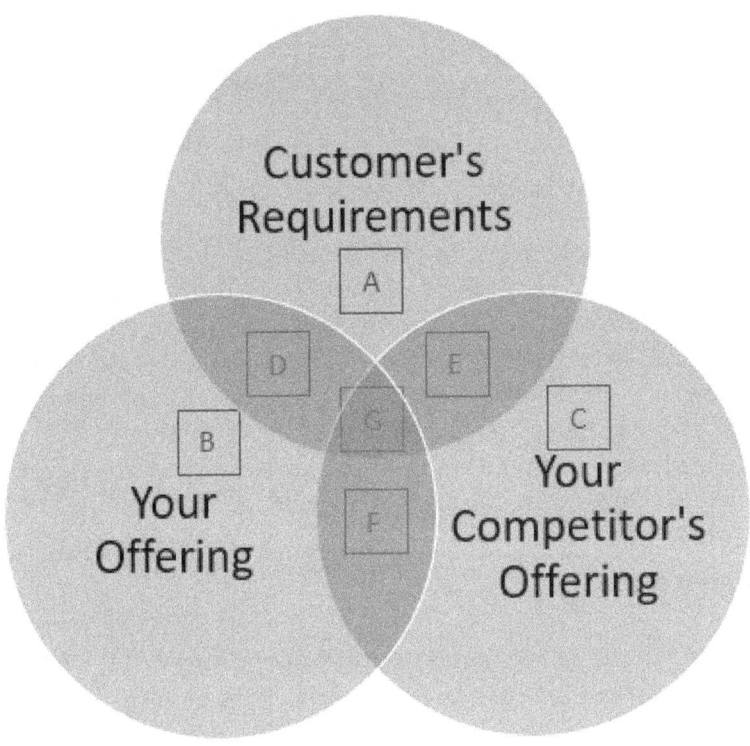

Figure 1: The Value Wedge - modified from source.

A. Your customer's requirements
B. The capabilities of your product or service
C. The capabilities of your competition's product or service
D. The customer requirements your product or service can deliver that your competitor cannot
E. The customer requirements your competition's product or service can deliver that yours cannot
F. The capabilities of your product or service that your competition shares

G. The customer requirements that you and your competition can deliver

How to leverage the value wedge

Knowing your competition is critical and so is understanding your customer's needs. Sit down with your buyer and fill this in, it will reveal what they understand about your competition as well as your own offering. I have used this tool many times as it allows me to have a real down-to-Earth conversation with my buyer about the state of their buying cycle. I can also dispel misconceptions of their view of my offering. Finally, I can use the opportunity to restate the value my offering would bring to the buyer and actually close the deal then and there.

They trust you

A seller cannot force a buyer into a decision. At one point in my career I had a boss who firmly believed he could sell anything to anyone. He would lose more than he won and when he did win it was always risky for the staff who must support the customer and deliver on the expectations set by our executive. Eventually he developed a reputation and people either loved or hated him. As an aside: he meant well, but his rough exterior was challenging for everyone who worked with him to deal with. The broader consequence is the impact on the customer.

He and I once were involved in a deal on the other side of the country. The buyer was struggling to understand what he was buying. One could argue it was a result of my boss's attempt to conceal precisely what was in the scope of the project. I was brought in to support the close of the deal towards the end of the selling cycle. My recommendation was to write an executive summary that explained the project scope in layman's terms. This is atypical. We closed the deal within days. Take note here: I did not play a Jedi mind trick on the buyer. I simply followed this principal.

Section 6: Asking Questions

Salespeople exist to drive revenue which triggers product creation and development. The most important function of a salesperson is to ask questions. We do not have to ask difficult questions at all, but they must be open-ended questions. A tool I was taught early in my career is called "STEWD". This is an acronym which stands for "share with me, tell me about, explain to me, walk me through and describe for me." Each of these open-ended requests elicits a different type of response from the answering party. Here is a breakdown:

Share with me

Sharing is caring, as my wife likes to remind our children. When you ask someone to "share" with you, you are suggesting that you care about their perspective and are willing to participate in solving the problem. This is a great way to build trust with your buyer.

Example) Share with me what it was like to work with our company the last time you were a customer.

Tell me about

Requesting someone *tell* you about a situation is a way of positioning yourself ready to provide help. You have been there before and you can provide council.

Example) Tell me about what happened that made you realize you have a problem.

Explain to me

With this request you are positioned as an authoritarian.

Example) Explain to me why you decided to use our competitor last time instead of us.

Walk me through

This is the request used when you want the buyer to provide an order of events.

Example) Walk me through what happened during your last software evaluation.

Describe for me

Use this request when you want details or a point of view.

Example) Describe for me the solution you are looking for.

Section 6: The Best Leads

While spending multiple hours weekly on existing opportunities a sales professional must continue to add future opportunities to their pipeline. Opportunities comes from many places: cold calling, email marketing, digital marketing and the personal network of the sales professional. The best leads come from trusted buyers – existing and past customers. I have maintained relationships with customers since my first year in sales. I can sell to them again and they provide me access to their professional network. A referral from a trusted buyer is more effective than simply picking up the phone and placing a cold call. I should also mention that I've built genuine friendships with many of my customers, which is a wonderful thing.

Developing new leads is something every seller should do every week. Accessing your personal network is difficult to scale as you are dependent on people understanding your value proposition, being in the network of your ideal buyers, and taking the time to introduce you. They are the best leads, but they are difficult to come by. Sellers must develop leads on their own as well. The following is an example of a high-level guide to cold lead development for business-to-business sales:

1. **Research**
    a. Read the company's social media posts and company reports such as 10Ks and 10Qs.
2. **Pre-Call**
    a. Warm them up before you call. First send a brief email informing the individual you will call them on a specific day and at a specific time.
    b. If they respond to your email by telling you to not call, respect their wish for now and move on to step 5.
    c. If they respond to a willingness for the call, see it through.
    d. If they do not respond, move on to step 3.
3. **First Cold Call**
    a. Place the call at the time you committed to. Make your reasons for reaching out to them crystal clear, every time.
    b. If you reach the contact, start by referencing the email you sent and confirming receipt. Your goal is to schedule a

meeting to better understand their need. That means you need to establish on this call if they have a need.
    c. If you do not reach the contact, leave a voice message and follow up with an email.
4. **Soft Touch**
    a. Reach out to the contact through LinkedIn.
    b. If you were unable to reach the contact before this point use this opportunity to let them know that you'd like to have a few minutes to discuss your product or service and that you will call them within a range of time (i.e. this afternoon). You may get a "not interested" reply which will save you the trouble of calling.
5. **Nurture Cycle**
    a. Repeat steps 3 and 4 at a reasonable pace until a meeting is scheduled or you are asked to stop reaching out. After a few attempts over a three to five-week period pause your efforts and reach out to another contact in the company.

Marketing Support

In my book *Marketing Operations- Make the Transformation* I outline in detail how digital marketing can create and qualify sales leads. A key principal from that book is the use of technology to capture analytical information that informs buyer behavior. Marketers can use this to filter inbound leads and then schedule appointments for the sales team. Marketers can also use it in outbound lead development with mass email and event-based demand generation. Again, any qualified lead would be sent to Sales for opportunity development. I have seen many salespeople become spoiled by great marketers. And when the well runs dry I've seen those salespeople lay goose eggs (not report any sales) months later because they did not continue to work their leads.

This technical and analytical practice can be leveraged directly by a seller as well. Sellers can send one thousand emails to a group of prospects and track if the contact opens an email, downloads the whitepaper you sent them or visits your website. That list of one thousand can be filtered down to the one hundred most active buyers who are most likely to be in a buying cycle. When the salesperson calls on this top one hundred they are being smarter with their time than cold calling the initial list of one thousand.

Decision Makers and Influencers

Knowing whom to call at every stage of the selling cycle is critical. A buyer with decision making authority is the ultimate contact to reach. This person holds the keys to your commission. I have seen salespeople struggle to close because they work exclusively with the influencers or informants and never reach the decision maker directly. To close the deal they rely on the friendly relationships they build with everyone but the decision maker. Great salespeople know how to gather information, gain mindshare within their target account and reach decision makers when it matters with qualified information before a proposal is delivered.

Decision informants

These are the end users that feel the pain the most. They are the analysts and generalists that must pull the levers and twist the knobs within the processes that are broken or inefficient.

Decision influencers

Influencers are the trusted advisors of decision makers. They can act within an organization as a manager or director.

Decision makers

Decisions can be made by an individual or a group.

Bottom up versus top down

There are two schools of thought regarding which layer in the decision-making hierarchy a salesperson should contact at the outset of their effort to gain access into an account. As a young sales professional I was afraid of titles. A never wanted to call or meet a CEO or CFO. I experienced less resistance and got more meetings with managers and end users. Management would jump on me about not having enough meetings "with the C suite." I had to change my approach to get them off my back. Over time I learned that directors and executives are not special. They are people just like us. Starting with the end users (influencers) or with the executives (decision makers) are both approaches with merit. So which one should you use? Well, it depends.

Bottom up

Starting at the bottom is good when you do not have access to anyone at the executive level. Between the end users and the executives is a sea of middle management whom may not have ultimate decision-making authority and do not have first-hand experience with the process and technology in place to help you understand the pain. The benefit of working through this method is a seller can gain tremendous information and work it upstream to managers, directors and executives. While working with each layer of management the seller is becoming a trusted advisor within the organization and has an opportunity to build a wide array of support, which decision makers may seek prior to making a final decision.

Top down

Starting at the top makes the most sense when there is either an existing relationship or a referral source that will introduce you to a decision maker. The goal from meeting with the decision maker is to gain sponsorship to work with the layers below and conduct a thorough analysis of their current state of technology, people and processes to ultimately formulate a value proposition.

Section 7: Now Go Win

There is no silver bullet for sellers. Even the greatest fisherperson who ever lived does not catch a fish without effort. Losing hurts. And sellers will lose. The best sellers I have worked with had one common trait that I believe was born from expecting they will lose some and win some. That trait is they did not celebrate their wins and they did not pout or blame others when they lost. Every great product has an alternative and you will find that your product may not be the most valuable for the buyer. When your buyer trusts you and they understand the value your offering can provide, it does not sting near as much when you lose. These sellers can go home knowing they gave it their best effort. And likely they did not lose the buyer as a contact down the road. There are many opportunities I have lost but later down the road I was able to earn their business after they gave the competition a shot to prove their value.

Below are my tips for staying motivated to put it all out there in every opportunity:

- Do not whine
- Do not put yourself in a position to blame others
- Find a mentor and a mentee
- Avoid negative people
- Choose a personal goal and justify your career towards that goal
- Outwork your competition
- Put yourself in the shoes of your buyer

Do not whine

I once went to a sales meeting without a notepad. The meeting went fine but afterward my manager expressed to me how disappointed he was with my decision. How could I possibly be a credible salesperson and not have the decency to show my customer that I care? My response was honest but whiney: "well there aren't any notebooks in the office." That response only made him more upset. Relative to my success, my choice to not use a notebook is not equivalent to missing a game winning jumper in game seven of the NBA finals. But my boss absolutely nailed it with his rebuttal: "go to the store and buy one." He was absolutely right. I should not deprive myself of a tool I need to do my job well. Whether or not I captured notes; his initial point was correct: my customer will not trust me if I do not show that I care. The whining did not do me any favors. Within a couple of months my position in that company was terminated. I have learned more from failing at that company than I can properly communicate in this book.

Do not put yourself in a position to blame others

Hard work does not always pay off immediately. When we lose, we lose because of a decision someone made to choose a competitor's offering. We are quickly up to two people we can blame for our loss. How about your manager? Or your sales engineer? Or that team lead from product development you brought along to help with your demo? Something I have learned along the way is the salesperson in any company is really a quarterback. It is their job to call the right play at the right time and to adjust if the play is not going according to plan. Blaming others does not change the outcome of the buyer's decision, but it does lose you points in the eyes of your team who trust you to call on them for the next deal.

Find a mentor and a mentee

Age does not matter but experience does. In every position I have held, save for one, I was always the youngest person on the sales team. Consequently, I have learned countless lessons from my more experienced peers. I built a few strong relationships along the way that continue to pay dividends with regard to my personal and professional development. These are not formal mentors – they are friends. Yet, the impact they have on me is like a mentor. After some reflection it was easy for me to see that I bring some value to them as well, even though I am more than ten years younger than they. In fact, my first sales manager is one of my dearest friends. He is twenty years older than I. Thus, it stands to reason that I have much to learn from someone younger than myself. We all do. And we also have something to give.

Avoid negative people

An underlying theme of this book is to be positive and find what motivates you. Being told "no" from buyers can be a hard thing to hear. It can give your stomach a sinking feeling and weigh on you for days. You will find abundant opportunity to air your grievances about your boss or a buyer to your colleagues. Every sales team I have been a part of has salespeople who wait for the phone to ring and paperwork to slide across their desk. They are not working hard, and management knows who they are. I have seen competent salespeople fall in with this crew. Shortly thereafter their numbers dropped. It is not a healthy path and it is difficult to work your way out of it.

Choose a personal goal and justify your career towards that goal

You should always have a goal. Visualizing your goal and setting milestones gives you the determination to deal with the grind of selling. The best salespeople I have worked with all had goals. I worked with an excellent salesperson whose territory was in a small market that I have also sold in. There were not many customers that fit the ideal buyer profile so he had to covet every deal he was in. He had two goals: to buy a vacation home that will eventually become his retirement home, and to buy an electric car to reduce his carbon footprint. These are great goals. In a difficult market where the reputation of his product had taken an unwarranted and public hit he was at a disadvantage. He had one of the best jobs a salesperson can have in this market so leaving for a situation that was better really was not an option. He built his territory plan and methodically worked his extended network to eventually land a few great sales and he accomplished the first of his two goals.

Outwork your competition

We live in a world full of distractions and when you are in a sales pursuit it is hard to not keep your eye squarely on winning when you also must grow your pipeline for the next fiscal quarter. For many salespeople winning one deal means they lost three to five. Although distraction is not the only thing to blame for a loss it is a common theme. And when we lose to someone else it is not always glaringly obvious that we were outworked. Energy exerted does not necessarily equate to winning percentage. A deal that you easily win is ripe for implementation and customer support issues. The one thing you can control is how hard you work. A manager once told me, "the quicker they come, the quicker they go." He is right. I have seen it time and time again when a colleague jumps for joy at a giant deal that came their way seemingly out of nowhere; only to lose it to a competitor just a few weeks later. Why did this happen? Usually it is because the buyer needed to challenge the competitor before the deal closed. Sometimes you can be surprised and win one of those deals. You can use the opportunity to identify the need and produce a compelling value proposition that changes the expected outcome. We call these "blue birds." And they are rare.

Put yourself in the shoes of your buyer

Would you buy this product or service? If it were your company, would you spend $100,000 on this? Should they trust you? These are just a few of the questions that should be going through the mind of a sales professional during their opportunity lifecycle. A principle I follow is from Jeffrey Gitomer's *The Little Red Book of Selling*. In it Gitomer writes regarding branding, "It is not who you know, it is who knows you." I've always taken this to mean the way I view myself I not necessarily how I am positioning myself to be perceived. In other words: I may think I'm trustworthy and my product is fantastic, but my prospective buyers may disagree.

CPSIA information can be obtained
at www.ICGtesting.com
Printed in the USA
LVHW090224160120
643822LV00001B/147